Hope
of the
Ages

Hope of the Ages

Compiled by
Nick Page

LION
Giftlines

This edition copyright © 1999 Lion Publishing

Published by
Lion Publishing plc
Sandy Lane West, Oxford, England
www.lion-publishing.co.uk
ISBN 0 7459 4204 0

First edition 1999
10 9 8 7 6 5 4 3 2 1 0

A catalogue record for this book is available
from the British Library

Typeset in 11/14 Caslon OldFace
Printed and bound in Singapore

What oxygen is to the lungs,
such is hope for the meaning of life.

Emil Brunner

Introduction

We need hope. St Paul, writing in the first century, identified faith, hope and love as the three great virtues. Without these, life is not worth living.

There are times, though, when hope can seem far away, and we long for comfort and reassurance. This book, beautifully illustrated with details from National Gallery fine art pictures, captures a spirit of hope drawn from 2,000 years of Christian experience.

Here is a message of comfort born of the suffering of many of the writers. Through their experiences, their thoughts and prayers, we are given fresh encouragement and hope. Their words have the power to lift us up and lead us on towards the hope of the world and the light of a new dawn.

The mystery of God

God moves in a mysterious way
his wonders to perform;
he plants his footsteps in the sea,
and rides upon the storm.

Deep in unfathomable mines
of never-failing skill
he treasures up his bright designs
and works his sovereign will.

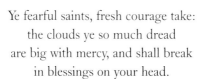

Ye fearful saints, fresh courage take:
the clouds ye so much dread
are big with mercy, and shall break
in blessings on your head.

William Cowper

Aelbert Cuyp, The Maas at Dordrecht in a Storm

Out of the depths

Heaven knows terrible things happen to people
in this world. The good die young, and the
wicked prosper, and in any one town, anywhere,
there is grief enough to freeze the blood. But
from deep within, whatever the hidden spring
is that life wells up from, there wells up into our
lives, even at their darkest, and maybe especially
then, a power to heal, to breathe new life into us.
And in this regard, I think, every person is a
mystic, because everyone at one time or another
experiences in the thick of joy or pain the power
out of the depths of life to bless.

Frederick Buechner

Do not be afraid

If you have a fearful thought, do not share it
with someone who is weak; whisper it to your
saddle-bow, and ride on singing.

King Alfred of Wessex

Netherlandish School,
The Magdalen Weeping

He is sufficient

Let nothing disturb you,
nothing frighten you;
all things are passing;
God never changes;
patient endurance
attains all things;
whoever possesses God
lacks nothing;
God alone suffices.

St Teresa of Avila

The rainbow

Oh joy that seekest me through pain,
I cannot close my eyes to thee:
I trace the rainbow through the rain,
and feel the promise is not vain,
that morn shall tearless be.

George Matheson

Georges Seurat,
The Rainbow

Real change

Hope alone is to be called 'realistic', because it alone takes seriously the possibilities with which all reality is fraught. It does not take things as they happen to stand or to lie, but as progressing, moving things with possibilities of change.

Jürgen Moltmann

Swallow's wings

True hope is swift, and flies with swallow's wings; kings it makes gods, and meaner creatures kings.

William Shakespeare

Sometimes

The sun will sometimes melt a field of sorrow that seemed hard frozen: may it happen for you.

Sheenagh Pugh

That special feeling

Hope is the feeling you have that the feeling
you have isn't permanent.

Jean Kerr

Master of Liesborn,
The Adoration of the Kings

Everyone sang

Everyone suddenly burst out singing;
and I was filled with such delight
as prisoned birds must find in freedom,
winging wildly across the white
orchards and dark-green fields;
on – on – and out of sight.

Everyone's voice was suddenly lifted;
and beauty came like the setting sun:
my heart was shaken with tears; and horror
drifted away… O, but Everyone
was a bird; and the song was wordless;
the singing will never be done.

Siegfried Sassoon

Do not cry

If you should hear that I have fallen in battle, do not cry. Remember that even the ocean in which my body sinks is only a pool in my Saviour's hand.

Anonymous German sailor, quoted by Helmut Thielicke

Gustave Courbet, Beach Scene

Love and peace

'After sharp showers,' said Peace,
'how shining the sun!
There's no weather warmer,
than after watery clouds.
Nor any love that has more delight,
nor friendship fonder,
than after war and woe,
when Love and Peace are the masters.

Never was war in this world,
nor wickedness so cruel,
but that Love, if he liked,
could bring all to laughing,
and Peace, through patience,
put stop to all perils.'

William Langland

Simon Denis, Sunset in the Roman Campagna

Point of view

Ah, Hope! What would life be, stripped of thy
encouraging smiles, that teach us to look behind
the dark clouds of today, for the golden beams
that are to gild the morrow.

Susannah Moodie

We are all in the gutter, but some of us are
looking at the stars.

Oscar Wilde

'Twixt optimist and pessimist
the difference is droll:
the optimist sees the doughnut;
the pessimist sees the hole.

Emily Dickinson

Girolamo da Carpi,
The Adoration of the Kings

A song of ascents

I lift up my eyes to the hills –
where does my help come from?
My help comes from the Lord,
the Maker of heaven and earth.

He will not let your foot slip –
he who watches over you will not slumber;
indeed, he who watches over Israel
will neither slumber nor sleep.

The Lord watches over you –
the Lord is your shade at your right hand;
the sun will not harm you by day,
nor the moon by night.

The Lord will keep you from all harm –
he will watch over your life;
the Lord will watch over your coming and going
both now and for evermore.

The Book of Psalms

Ary Scheffer,
Saints Augustine and Monica

Possibilities

When one door of happiness closes, another opens; but often we look so long at the closed door that we do not see the one which has been opened for us.

Helen Keller

If you do not hope, you will not find out what is beyond your hopes.

St Clement of Alexandria

Rise up

Be patient with everyone, but above all with yourself. I mean, do not be disheartened by your imperfections, but always rise up with fresh courage.

St Francis of Sales

Just remember – when you think all is lost, the future remains.

Robert Goddard

Giovanni Battista Piazzetta,
The Sacrifice of Isaac

The three virtues

I am, God says, Master of the Three Virtues...

It is Faith who holds fast
through century after century.
It is Charity who gives herself
through centuries of centuries,
but it is my little hope
who gets up every morning...

It is Faith who watches
through centuries of centuries.
It is Charity who watches
through centuries of centuries.
But it is my little hope
who lies down every evening
and gets up every morning
and really has very good nights...

Charles Péguy

Lippo di Dalmasio,
The Madonna of Humility

Hope of the years

O little town of Bethlehem,
how still we see thee lie!
Above thy deep and dreamless sleep
the silent stars go by.
Yet in thy dark streets shineth
an everlasting light;
the hopes and fears of all the years
are met in thee tonight.

Phillips Brooks

Giovanni Battista Pittoni,
The Nativity with God the Father and the Holy Ghost

The awakening of life

When hope does awaken, an entire life awakens along with it. One comes fully to life. It begins to seem indeed that one has never lived before. One awakens to a life that is eternal in prospect, a life that opens up before one all the way to death and beyond, a life that seems able to endure death and survive it. Wherever hope rises, life rises.

John S. Dunne

Change the world

That is the hope that inspires Christians. We know that every effort to better society, especially when injustice and sins are so ingrained, is an effort that God blesses, that God wants, that God demands of us.

Oscar Romero

Bernardo Cavallino,
Christ Driving the Traders from the Temple

Nothing can separate us

I am convinced that there is nothing in death or life… nothing in all creation that can separate us from the love of God in Christ Jesus our Lord.

St Paul the Apostle

Life in death

The joy of God has been through the poverty of the crib and the distress of the cross; therefore it is insuperable, irrefutable. It does not deny the distress where it is, but finds God in the midst of it, indeed precisely there; it does not contest the most grievous sin, but finds forgiveness in just this way; it looks death in the face, yet finds life in death itself.

Dietrich Bonhoeffer

Peter Paul Rubens,
The Coup de Lance

The promised land

I've been to the mountain top. And I've looked over, and I've seen the promised land… I'm not fearing any man. Mine eyes have seen the glory of the coming of the Lord.

Martin Luther King Jr

The eternal vision

The idea of heaven is the legacy of the most radical and most central hope. Heaven is the central and innermost significance of everything that man has ever hoped.

Ladislaus Boros

Hope is the struggle of the soul, breaking loose from what is perishable, and attesting her eternity.

Herman Melville

Francisque Millet,
Mountain Landscape, with Lightning

Farther up and farther in

The difference between the old Narnia and the new Narnia was like that. The new one was a deeper country: every rock and flower and blade of grass looked as if it meant more. I can't describe it any better than that: if you ever get there you will know what I mean.

It was the Unicorn who summed up what everyone was feeling. He stamped his right forehoof on the ground and neighed and then cried:

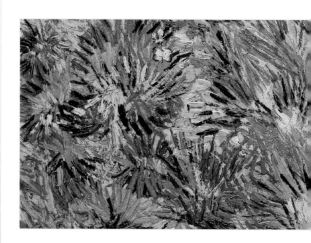

'I have come home at last! This is my real country! I belong here. This is the land I have been looking for all my life, though I never knew it till now. The reason why we loved the old Narnia is that it sometimes looked a little like this… Come farther up and farther in!'

C.S. Lewis

Vincent van Gogh, Long Grass with Butterflies

Up-hill

Does the road wind up-hill all the way?
Yes, to the very end.
Will the day's journey take the whole long day?
From morn to night, my friend.

But is there for the night a resting-place?
A roof for when the slow dark hours begin.
May not the darkness hide it from my face?
You cannot miss that inn.

Shall I meet other wayfarers at night?
Those who have gone before.
Then must I knock, or call when just in sight?
They will not keep you standing at that door.

Shall I find comfort, travel-sore and weak?
Of labour you shall find the sum.
Will there be beds for me and all who seek?
Yea, beds for all who come.

Christina Rossetti

Nicolas Poussin,
Landscape in the Roman Campagna

The task

We are a pilgrim people, a people who have
decided never to arrive, a people who live by
hope, energized not by what we already possess,
but by that which is promised: 'Behold, I create
a new heaven and a new earth.'

Sure, it's tiring and it's tough. Imagination
comes harder than memory, and faithfulness is
more demanding than success. But so what if
we fail? Remember, we are not required to finish
the task – any more than we are allowed to put
it aside.

William Sloane Coffin

Pieter Lastman,
The Rest on the Flight into Egypt

The pilgrimage of hope

Give me my scallop-shell of quiet,
my staff of faith to walk upon,
my scrip of joy, immortal diet,
my bottle of salvation,
my gown of glory, hope's true gage,
and thus I'll take my pilgrimage.

Walter Raleigh

Attributed to Bartolomé Esteban Murillo,
St John the Baptist in the Wilderness

Let's dance

You may dance the tune played by the present reality. Your style of life will be realistic and pragmatic. Or you may choose to move your body under the spell of a mysterious tune and rhythm which come from a world we do not see, the world of our hopes and aspirations. Hope is hearing the melody of the future. Faith is to dance it.

Rubem A. Alves

Lorenzo Costa,
The Story of Moses (The Dance of Miriam)

Welcome, day!

The last words of Mr Despondency were,
Farewell, night; welcome, day!
His daughter went through the river singing,
but none could understand what she said.

John Bunyan

The final blessing

All shall be well, and all shall be well,
and all manner of things shall be well.

Julian of Norwich

Ambrosius Benson,
The Magdalen Reading

Text acknowledgments

14: 'Sometimes' from *Selected Poems*, copyright © 1990 Sheenagh Pugh, published by
Seren Books, Poetry Wales Press. Used by permission of the author. 16: 'Everyone
Sang', copyright © 1920 by E.P. Dutton, copyright renewed 1948 by Siegfried
Sassoon, from *Collected Poems of Siegfried Sassoon* by Siegfried Sassoon. Used by kind
permission of George Sassoon and of Viking Penguin, a division of Penguin Putnam
Inc. 22: Psalm 121, quoted from the *Holy Bible, New International Version*, copyright
© 1973, 1978, 1984 by International Bible Society. Used by permission. 32: Romans
8:38–39, quoted from the Revised English Bible, copyright © 1989 Oxford
University Press and Cambridge University Press. 36: extract taken from *The Last
Battle*, C.S. Lewis, published by HarperCollins Publishers Ltd.

Picture acknowledgments

All pictures are copyright © The National Gallery, London.

Cover: NG 3091 The Virgin and Child with Four Saints (detail), Francesco
Bonsignori. 8–9: NG 6405 The Maas at Dordrecht in a Storm (detail), Aelbert
Cuyp. 10–11: NG 3116 The Magdalen Weeping (detail), Netherlandish School.
12–13: NG 6555 The Rainbow (detail), Georges Seurat. 14–15: NG 258 The
Adoration of the Kings (detail), Master of Liesborn. 16–17: NG 6396 Beach Scene
(detail), Jean-Désiré-Gustave Courbet. 18–19: NG 6562 Sunset in the Roman
Campagna (detail), Simon Denis. 20–21: NG 640 The Adoration of the Kings
(detail), Girolamo da Carpi. 22–23: NG 1170 Saints Augustine and Monica
(detail), Ary Scheffer. 24–25: NG 3163 The Sacrifice of Isaac (detail), Giovanni
Battista Piazzetta. 26–27: NG 752 The Madonna of Humility (detail), Lippo di
Dalmasio. 28–29: NG 6279 The Nativity with God the Father and the Holy Ghost
(detail), Giovanni Battista Pittoni. 30–31: NG 4778 Christ Driving the Traders from
the Temple (detail), Bernardo Cavallino. 32–33: NG 1865 The Coup de Lance
(detail), Peter Paul Rubens. 34–35: NG 5593 Mountain Landscape, with Lightning
(detail), Francisque Millet. 36–37: NG 4169 Long Grass with Butterflies (detail),
Vincent van Gogh. 38–39: NG 6391 Landscape in the Roman Campagna (detail),
Nicolas Poussin. 40–41: L 162 The Rest on the Flight into Egypt (detail), Pieter
Lastman. 42–43: NG 3938 St John the Baptist in the Wilderness (detail), attributed
to Bartolomé Esteban Murillo. 44–45: NG 3104 The Story of Moses (The Dance
of Miriam) (detail), Lorenzo Costa. 46–47: NG 655 The Magdalen Reading
(detail), Ambrosius Benson.